DEAR _____,
THERE'S HOPE
ON THE
OTHER SIDE

Lisa M. Godwin

ISBN 978-1-0980-2727-8 (paperback)
ISBN 978-1-0980-2728-5 (digital)

Christian Faith Publishing, Inc.
832 Park Avenue
Meadville, PA 16335
www.christianfaithpublishing.com

Printed in the United States of America

Introduction

My life has not been typical by any means. What I mean by this is life has looked very different for me than any other person I have met. Growing up in the home I was raised in was not easy. I've had many people respond to me sharing my story by saying, "It can't get much worse than that." The truth is yes, it can, and it does for some. Maybe that person is you.

No matter what your struggles are in life, and no matter what your life choices have been, one thing in this life remains true and constant—Jesus! You may not have any idea who He is, and that is okay. By the time you are done reading these letters, I hope you not only have an idea of who He is, but I hope He becomes your Savior, Lord, and life. He is the treasure I found at a really dark time in my life, and I will never go back to the way I was before I found this treasure and before I understood what it looked like to exchange my ugly sinful life for His perfect sinless life that He sacrificed on the cross for me. This is a concept that I will explain further in the pages of this book so you can understand how this can take place for you as well. For me, it became a lifestyle. The life Jesus offers is what sustains me, guides me, loves me, and gives me life beyond measure. There is no one and nothing in this world that can compare to Him. If we decide to put our faith in his hands, there is no one who will love us more, forgive us more, give us more grace and mercy than Jesus Christ. He is all of this, and so much more.

Please understand, this treasure I found in Jesus didn't come as a result of doing the right things all the time, looking like I live a perfect life, or pleasing everyone around me. The treasure I found in Jesus was something I had to search for with all of my heart. Just like a hidden treasure, it takes effort and persistence to find, but once you come upon it, you can celebrate what you've found. You can enjoy the results of all of your hard work. It seems the same way with this treasure. When you finally find Jesus and all that He offers, you will rest with peace, knowing no matter what you do, He will never stop loving you. What I mean by this is that once you confess your sins and believe on the name of Jesus and all that He did on the cross, you become His child. You can't earn your salvation, so you don't need to strive to earn His love. He loves you as much as He ever will. We can now enjoy having a relationship with him through reading the Bible and studying what it means, spending time in prayer with Him, and trusting in His will for our lives. We (I) need to realize He was the only one that could meet all of my needs all of the time. He knows me better than anyone and yet He chooses to love me and forgive me, and that is amazing!

What is even more amazing about this treasure I've found in Him is that He creates in me the ability to see others as He sees them. He freely forgives everyone for their sins as a result of Him dying on the cross for our sins. He takes joy in watching His children forgiving one another, much like a parent takes joy in watching their own children forgive each other and live in peace together. I am thankful He gives me the ability to forgive and love beyond what I have the capacity to do as a human. This is an example of exchanging my unforgiving and selfish heart for His heart of love. The treasure in Jesus didn't just change my identity (who I am) but my outlook, my mission, and my response to life and the circumstances it brings.

I am choosing not to keep quiet any longer. God has done an amazing work in my life. I am in great anticipation of the future He holds for me and you as you read these letters. So many times, I have thought that maybe it is not the right time to share my story. I wonder what people would think of me if I did share my story. I have prayed and asked God to show me His will and His timing. He gave me an answer, and I believe it's time. I am stepping out of my comfort zone with courage. I pray you will do the same in what God is calling you to do in obedience. I'm not going to allow Satan to discourage me from sharing any longer.

Please understand, this is not just about my story, but it's about God's story within my story, and I hope you will see this in the next few pages. I am not the same person I was years ago, and I will never be the same since I found the treasure of Jesus. My hope and prayer is that you will be encouraged by what I have written and that you will be challenged to seek Jesus with all of your heart, mind, and soul. It's your choice to join me as a treasure hunter and a truth seeker. Don't think it's not for you, or that you will never find it. That is a lie from the enemy who wants to get in the way of you having a relationship with God. God is enough for everyone that truly seeks Him!

I currently have a job where I have the privilege of empowering women who have hit rock bottom in life or are well on their way. I work at a women and children's homeless shelter. Accepting this job was a result of healing from the hardships life has thrown my way. As a result, I am writing this book in the form of letters to all the ladies who have gone through my shelter or ladies who are feeling hopeless and traumatized by what life has thrown their way. Our struggles, though they may look different in nature, have the same solutions. These are truths that I encourage them with every day. I believe that God's amazing work in my life is for a purpose, and that is to encourage and empower others who are in desperate need of it. Someone once told me that I am like a "shiny penny." Well, hopefully, sharing my story will demonstrate how it doesn't matter where or what you've come from; we can all be shiny pennies. The key to this is Jesus! My hope for you is that the words on the following pages will both encourage you and empower you to run every day to Jesus and to cling to Him. I encourage you to open up your heart and listen to His truths.

Letter 1

*D*ear Idolater,

Please don't give in to idolatry. When I think about my relationship with Jesus and the activities, people, or desires that get in the way of my fellowship with Him, it's hard for me not to call them idols. Sometimes, they've become idols with me not realizing that's what they've become. Your idols may look very different than my idols, but the bottom line is that they always create distance between us and God. Many times, I find myself desiring to spend time with friends or family rather than spending time reading the Bible and praying. Please understand that spending time with family or talking with them on the phone is not a bad thing, but when we would rather talk to them and spend more time with them than God, it is a problem. It is so easy, for me especially, to rely heavily on people for answers to my problems or to meet my needs instead of allowing God to do this for me. He wants to be the desire of our hearts, but this can only happen through making our relationship with Him a priority.

At times, I go through periods in my life where I get addicted to certain television programs. All I want to do when I get home from a hard day at work is watch the latest movie series I am into. Instead of spending time with family and having my personal quiet time with God, I find myself staring at a television for hours on end. This is a perfect example of the way the enemy works to separate us from having a strong, consistent relationship with God. Think about it this way. If you were married and spend zero time with your spouse, you would lose track of who they are and what they desire. You may even start to feel isolated from them and seek out other methods of getting your needs met because they are not being met by your spouse.

Another example is my obsession with a clean house, free from messes and clutter. My husband, children, and close friends would attest to the fact that perfectionism was an idol for me. When our family would invite guests over to our home, I would spend hours upon hours making sure the entire house was clean. We could pretty much eat off of the bathroom floor. When relatives would come from out of town to stay with us, my husband and children would have to prepare themselves for the emotional meltdown I would have along the way of making sure everything in the house was clean and neat. I was so concerned about what our guests thought of me as a house cleaner than anything else. It ruled my life for many years, and it created misery in our home. Once I let go of the perfectionism and realized that having a clean house didn't make me a better person or worthy to be loved, I experienced freedom. No longer was perfectionism an idol in my life.

In my opinion, idolatry is like a chain hanging on us. We drag it everywhere we go, and it wears us down. Once we can identify our idols, we can confess them to God as our sins and move on, without those heavy chains weighing us down.

Living in our first world country, with so much at our fingertips, brings opportunity for us to struggle with idolatry. We have to be on guard and keep it in check. Satan is our enemy, and the enemy obviously uses this to separate us from God. He is pleased when we become distracted with what has been created versus focusing on the creator Himself, God. This is a challenge we all have to come to grips with. God wants to intervene and save us from ourselves. He wants to help us navigate through life. What we think would be good for us might actually get in the way of our relationship with God, and if we are not careful, it can become an idol.

Many times, we think that having lots of money will get rid of all of our problems. This is a lie. The truth is, the more money and things we own, the more we may struggle with self-sufficiency. When we have everything we physically need and aren't dependent on anyone or anything else for our needs to be met, we risk losing our faith in God, who we should be fully dependent on for everything. Then think about it this way. What happens when you receive a call from a loved one that just received a grim diagnosis from their doctor. Your perspective becomes very different. You realize you are not in control, and your self-sufficiency begins to diminish. You are now dependent on doctors, nurses and, ultimately, God's plan for your loved one. Your faith is forced to grow. I have experienced this scenario firsthand with my oldest brother who was diagnosed with cancer. There was nothing I could do but pray. I had to trust that God would take care of him. Especially because I lived 3,000 miles away and could literally do nothing.

When I was a young girl, I used to dream a lot, and let me explain why and what this has to do with idolatry. I had a father who was addicted to pornography and was soliciting my mom for sex. They would leave our house after my brothers and I went to sleep for the night and be gone until the morning. Sometimes, as young children, my older brother and I would wake up in the morning and get ready for school on our own. We would spend time sitting in front of the living room window waiting for our parents to get home so we could go to school. We were both in elementary school, and our younger brother was still a baby, so we knew we couldn't leave him home alone. You can imagine all of the dysfunctions that began to occur in our home due to the unwanted guest—pornography. It was an idol that my dad had allowed in his life. I believed it meant more to him than I did. He was willing to sacrifice everything for it. At a very young age, I knew what they were doing and prayed to God they would stop. It didn't stop until I was a senior in high school. Most of my childhood was spent with this unwanted guest ruling our home. I hated it and wanted it to prey on someone else's home, but it had no intentions of leaving. It made itself nice and comfortable and was there to stay. Along with the sexual addiction came physical abuse and emotional abuse. You are probably wondering if it was ever done to me. The answer is no. God protected me in so many ways. My name actually means "consecrated to God." I believe that, at age five, when I asked Jesus to be my Lord and Savior and confessed my sins to Him, my life was consecrated to Him.

I share this story for you to see that, sometimes, our own issues of idolatry directly affect those around us. It especially affects those who are close to us. As a child, I attempted to navigate through the insecurity that was brought on by my dad's sexual addiction. I was afraid every night before I went to bed. I wanted my parents to hurry up and leave for the night so I could fall asleep. Many times, my mom would not want to go, and my dad would use physical force to get her out of the house. This only created fear of my dad in me. I would sleep with my head fully hidden under the blanket so it would muffle the sound of the abuse. As a young child, I mustered up the courage to ask my dad why they were going out at night, and he responded by telling me to mind my own business. I was in fifth grade when I finally figured it all out. Up until this point, I just thought my parents were working on a surprise for us kids. I honestly thought they were working on getting us a motor home so we could travel on vacation together. This was how my naive little seven-year-old mind worked. Wow, was I ever disappointed when I realized what was really happening. You can only imagine how disappointed I was.

This was when the idolatry started for me. My emotional needs were not being met by my parents, and I was still learning about who God is, so I turned to other idols that I thought could fill those voids. I am sure you have voids that you are trying to fill that only God can fill through having a relationship with Him. He wants to fill them and will if you ask Him, and if you trust Him. It's amazing to me how young I was when I began seeking idols. We don't need to be taught how to do this, but we do need to be taught how to undo the idols in our lives. I would like to share with you another example of an idol I fed in my life.

I remember in elementary school, I would go to school and sit in class wondering how it would feel to be a kid whose parents stayed home all night long. The security I would have felt was overwhelming for me to think about. I would also wonder what it would be like to live in a home where there was no arguing and fighting. I can honestly say that this was when my love affair with the idols of security and comfort started. I desired it so much it hurt. I just wanted to be like all of my friend's families. I wanted to see my parents show love for each other. I wanted to know what it felt like to be provided for and not worry about money. I wanted to experience peace in our home and not feel anxiety every time my dad walked through the door. I wanted to know what it would be like to make a mistake and not spend hours listening to the lectures. I wanted to know what it would be like to not worry about my parents divorcing. From my perspective, it seemed like all my classmates had such peaceful, happy lives. Sure they had their small issues to deal with from time to time, but nothing close to what I had to deal with on a daily basis when I would walk through the back door of my house. My friends had no idea how good they had it and knew nothing about what I was going through.

As you can imagine, with a guest like this running our home, money became scarce. We were no longer a middle-class family. My parents were struggling to make ends meet, and it was affecting every area of our life. We moved from house to house because we were renting all the time. My parents also had to walk away from a home they had purchased because they could no longer afford it. We were living in less than desirable neighborhoods. I felt like a fish out of water, but I also felt like a fish out of water at the Christian school we attended because many of the families were wealthy. I was desperately seeking acceptance from somewhere. I definitely didn't feel accepted at home by my parents. Again, I started to desire what some of my friends had. I was so desperate for relief from what was happening in our home that I became a solid worshipper of the "god of comfort." In fact, I could have been the pastor at this "Church of Comfort" if it actually existed. It wasn't until I was in my thirties that I realized this was a problem in my life, and I needed to get rid of this false god of comfort and replace it with the true God. I realize we all desire comfort. However, when it becomes such a strong desire that we are willing to do anything to get it, it becomes an idol. It is replacing God. The enemy knew how badly I wanted relief from my pain and comfort through love and acceptance, and he was continually trying to discourage me.

Out of this desperate search for comfort grew many sins from declaring my will over God's will in my life. I was going to live my life very different from the way my parents lived theirs. I was going to make very different decisions than what they made. I decided and declared I was never going to go into bankruptcy or lose a home. I was going to marry well, be actively involved in my church, and I was never going to leave my kids home alone at night. I was always going to give them love and security as best as I could. I was also going to go to college to get an education, which would hopefully lead to a good job. All of these declarations I made would provide me with a safe, secure, and worry-free life with money, security, love, etc. I believed the lie that I could accomplish this no matter what. While these items are not bad in and of themselves, the desire to get them at any cost without checking to see if this is God's will for my life was wrong. It was flat out sin, and this sin was separating me from having not just a relationship with God but fellowship with Him as well. I was declaring my will over His will. Later on in life, He showed me what His will really was for me. To no surprise, it was very different from what I thought it would be.

Declaring the way I wanted my life to go gave me the wrong notion that I was the one in charge of my life and that I determined my own footsteps. I learned later on in life that true security comes from understanding Proverbs 16:9 that states, "We can make our plans, but the Lord determines our steps." This was so true, and this verse brought me comfort when I decided to finally submit to God and His will for my life. I was trying to get peace and comfort from things outside of Jesus, but God had something to say about it, and I am so thankful. His total sovereignty provides total comfort to those who choose to have faith in it. The "little god of comfort" pales in comparison to the maker of the universe and the lover of our souls, Jesus Christ. He alone is all we need to bring us comfort.

There's a story in the Bible that often reminds me of the distraction of idolatry, and it is the story found in the Bible in the book of Genesis. Moses was on the mountain meeting with God for forty days and forty nights. In the meantime, the Israelites were getting restless, waiting for Moses to come down off the mountain, so they went ahead and built an idol. They collected gold and created a golden calf to worship. Every time I read this story, I think to myself, *Are you kidding me. You can't even be patient for forty days. You push forward and make another idol to worship instead.* It was easier for them to build the idol than to trust God. Isn't this the same thing we do as well? We get impatient waiting on God, or we dislike how he determined life should go, so we take it into our own hands. We are really no different than the Israelites, and I can honestly say I have done this many times. It is not easy to have faith in God's truth, especially when we have to wait. We struggle with that which is uncomfortable instead of embracing it as an opportunity for spiritual growth. I am so very thankful for God's continued patience with us as His people.

When I made these claims of what I wanted my life to look like, I was a professed believer and follower of Jesus. I had grown up in church and accepted Jesus as my Lord and

Savior. Our family attended church until my parents were thrown out of the church for their continual sexual sin. I remember sitting in the pew with my older brother, listening to our parent ask for forgiveness, and because they continued to go out at night, we couldn't go back to church. So we stopped attending church, but to my surprise, my parents enrolled me into a Christian school. I was being fed truths about who I was in Christ by my teachers and through attending chapel once a week. However, even though I knew Jesus was my Savior, I was really struggling with Him being my life. I clung to Him for peace in my life, but I also tried to take control of it as well. I was determined to push my personal life agenda forward just the way I wanted to, and no one was in my life to tell me any different. So full steam ahead. I was determined to earn the respect of people and not be a product of my childhood. I was not going to let my parents' behavior dictate who I would be as an adult. I was going to change the trajectory of my life, and I was pretty sure God was going to step back and let me since I was striving to make good choices in my life. I had a lot to learn about works-based acceptance from God. It is not about what we can do for Him; it is about loving Him with all of our being, and the rest will follow. God was very gracious and gentle with me as He taught me His truths. I am so very thankful to Him for this.

Please know that you don't have to live your life in misery because you think you need to control your life. It seems as if the tighter you hold on, the more misery and stress you will experience. Instead, spend time with Jesus in prayer, seek Godly counsel, and let Him lead you to what He has for you. No matter what you may think your life should look like, he knows what's best. We can depend on His sovereignty as well as his omniscience (the fact that He knows everything). He knows what His plans are for you in the future and what you need right now because He created you. He knows what is good for you and what you can and can't handle. This should bring you so much comfort, security, and peace. Don't give in to the lie that life has to be comfortable, and if we are uncomfortable then something must be wrong with us, or we've made poor decisions. We should be focused on the example of Jesus's life when He was here on earth. He made the choice to live as a servant instead of choosing to live as a king in a comfortable palace. He knew why He was here on earth and kept his focus on obedience to God. What makes us think we are any better than Jesus to live a comfortable life? I encourage you to begin to embrace these truths at a practical, everyday level, and challenge yourself to change your thinking. It isn't easy, but it will definitely produce spiritual fruit!

Letter 2

*D*ear Worthy,

You are worth much! It doesn't matter what you have done or not done in the past, you are loved by the God who created everything in the universe. I understand that many people in your life have said and done hurtful things to you. It doesn't change your worth to God. I understand that you have done things in your life that you are ashamed of and that our enemy, Satan, would like to use these things to separate you from having relationship with God. However, this does not change your worth to God. He will never love you more than He loves you now. God has a specific plan for your life, and He offers healing to you—healing from what others have said and done to hurt you, and healing from the consequences of choices you have made. Your part in all of this is to remove the curtain that is hanging in front of your hurts and expose them to God's truth. You have to be willing to pull the hurts and pain out of the dark to let God's light shine on them. I found this truth in 1 John 1:7 which states, "But if we walk in the light, as he is in the light, we have fellowship with one another, and the blood of Jesus, his Son, purifies us from all sin".

Once God provides healing, the hurts are now protected by Him, so don't give in to the lie that says you really are not healed. Give God total access to your hurts and then claim the healing He brings to you. The reason I know and believe this is because I have personally experienced His amazing healing and also because His name means Jehovah Rapha—the God who heals. This God who heals can and will do this if you make yourself vulnerable and let Him in. One way to do this is found further in the chapter of 1 John 1. In verses 8–9, it states, "If we claim to be without sin, we deceive ourselves and the truth is not in us. If we confess our sins, he is faithful and just and will forgive us our sins and purify us from all unrighteousness." It is not easy, my friend, to confess and bring our sin up and exposed to the light. Along with exposing this, we have to realize we are not our sin. Our sin is not our identity; Jesus is. He gives us our worth. Coming to grips with this is not an easy task. Nothing that is worth anything is easy. But if I can do it, so can you. It takes intentional thinking and effort on our part to believe truth.

One of the ways I've lived in my true worth is I had to separate what others have done to me and said to hurt me from how much God loves me. I had to stop blaming God for the behavior of His people He created. God is not man. He is truly our heavenly Father and loves us with a perfect love that only a heavenly Father can love with. I needed to work toward lowering my expectations of people and realize they are not perfect, and never will be. I had to realize they will hurt me, and they will fail me (even if they don't intend to). This is just part of our life here on earth. Also, I had to learn to exercise forgiveness in the light of the fact that I want to be forgiven. I know I will hurt other people, either intentionally or not as well, and I surely want them to forgive me. How can I expect others to forgive me if I myself am not willing to forgive? This is something I had to mull over for a long time, and when I finally came to the conclusion through the truths of Scripture, I needed to stop holding everyone else accountable for every wrong action they ever did to me. I had to embrace the act of forgiveness along with realizing the Bible is clear that I am not to judge others. I am supposed to let God be the judge. This decision alone brought me so much freedom. This alone allows me to live in my true worth and the freedom I had been searching for so long. You see, I have enough of a burden keeping track of my own sins in order to confess. Why would I want to keep track of every-one else's sin? Not to mention, it's a waste of time since I can't confess them on their behalf anyway.

I learned to not let what other people say or do to me distract me from what God says about me. The enemy likes to use this as a distraction from the truth that we are God's children. We are joint heirs with Jesus. God sees us as being worthy enough to be His child and coheirs or equals to Christ. Our position is in Him, and Him in us—incredible! This means that nothing can happen to us without it going through God first. You might ask, "Then why does He let bad things happen to good people?" I can't answer this because I know that in Isaiah 55:8–9 it states, "For my thoughts are not your thoughts, neither are your ways my ways, declares the Lord." As I mentioned earlier, God is all-knowing, and that alone should bring us peace and comfort. I believe that

God either causes things to happen or allows them to happen. This basically means God is sovereign. He is over all things. So many things in my life have happened that just don't make any sense. These events could have caused me to turn away from the Lord. However, I have chosen to trust God's character, not my circumstances. I choose to trust God's goodness, rather than other people's opinions of me. I chose to let my heavenly Father dictate my worth.

This was a hard lesson for me to learn. When I began going to college, I lived under the assumption that I could control how other people felt about me. Because I believed this, I could control whether or not they would like me. Again, another lie I believed, served up on a platter from the enemy. In my mind, this would eliminate people from saying or doing anything that would hurt me. Especially if they call themselves a "Christian" and said they were my friends and cared about me. It all boiled down to me turning into a people pleaser. I decided if I could please all people, no matter what it cost me, then life would be comfortable. If I could get along with everyone, I would feel worthy to be loved and accepted. This most certainly didn't happen in my home growing up. At a very young age, I did not feel worthy enough to be loved. The messages I received from extended family, friends, and the church was that I was not worth saving, and I was not worth being uncomfortable for. You see, no one came to my rescue while living in a dysfunctional home. No one cared to see the warning signs of hurt, anger, and abuse. That translated into the message that I was not worthy of loving. When I graduated from high school, I decided I was going to do everything I could to be accepted by everyone, even my parents. I would take control. I was done with rejection. You see, I never really felt accepted even from my parents. I felt as if I was not good enough to provide for or work hard for because we didn't have much, and money was always an issue. I believed what I had to say didn't matter because my parents didn't listen to me and how I was feeling about all of the dysfunction happening in our family. They simply made the assumption that I was fine. However, I believed I had no voice. Because they chose to focus solely on their own needs and meeting them anyway they felt they could, it didn't matter how their decisions were affecting my brothers and I. We could not share how we felt and, instead, had to suppress our anger and our frustration with the way life was for us. More than anything, I wanted to feel truly accepted and loved by my parents. I wanted to feel like I was worth being loved.

What I didn't realize is that I was accepted by God and had a voice that he gave me. I was worth dying for on the cross. I was worth Christ rising from the dead on the third day, and I am worth Him giving me eternal life so I can live forever with my heavenly Father in heaven. I made a deliberate decision to understand that my worth is not in who my parents are, or what they did. My worth is not based on who my friends are, or what they think of me. It's not even what I have done to deserve another person's condemnation. My worth is in Jesus. I love in 1 Corinthians 2:2 where Paul states, "For I resolved to know nothing while I was with you except Jesus Christ and Him crucified." Paul understood that his entire worth was in Christ Jesus. This worth is not just for Paul, but we should be encouraged by his words as well. If he can live in the worth of who Jesus is, so can we. This is part of the treasure of Christ's life available to us.

Not feeling good enough or worthy to be loved or cared for is a lie that we need to repel in our minds. We are good enough, and we need to let others know they are good enough too. In today's society, it seems like we are in competition all the time to be better than everyone else. We try to succeed in every area of life because we believe that will make us feel good enough. We tend to live off our feelings—which seems to change every other minute. Instead of focusing on whether or not we feel like we measure up to everyone else, how about we accept the truth that is in us that states we are good enough. How about we focus our attention on helping those around us feel like they are worthy of love and acceptance through the Word of truth. Instead of living in a bubble of constant insecurity about ourselves, how about we live in the security of our salvation and our relationship with God and then yield to being a tool God can use to help move others to do the same. Think of the work we could do building God's kingdom if we focused more on other's needs than our own. Even as believers, we have become so self-focused instead of God focused. Let's stop obsessing about getting out own needs met and live to build God's kingdom for His glory.

Once I came to the realization it is not my job to please everyone, I was able to set boundaries in relationships that were unhealthy. We rarely realize how important setting appropriate boundaries with people in our life is to our spiritual health. This behavior intentionally creates an environment where God now has center stage and can move and work without our interference. We removed the idol of other people and placed God where He always should have been, and that is at the center of all we do. Sometimes, our need to fix other people or get involved in other people's lives can create more problems instead of us being helpful. When we step over the boundary line and try to be God in someone else's life, we run the risk of causing them to put their trust in us instead of God. We need to step out of the way so God can be God in someone else's life. This was a lesson that took many years for me to learn. My desire to people please and help was a blind spot that needed to be addressed. This was especially true when it came to my parents. I was always running to the rescue whenever they needed help. They would call me for encouragement when they were down, money when they needed it, and everything else that they thought I could fix. It wasn't until recently that I realized my job was to point them to Christ. My job was not to provide for them; that was God's job. Sometimes, the most beneficial action we can do for someone else is nothing. When I gave the burden of fixing my parent's problems over to the Lord and determined to stop being their god that they can trust, it was so freeing. I stopped carrying a burden that was never mine to carry in the first place. I was also able to realize the only person I need to worry about pleasing is God. When I am in right relationship with Him, it frees me to love others unconditionally in the same way He loves me. Whether they accept my gift of love is up to them. Some may accept it, and some may not. I have realized that it is okay if some people don't accept my gift of love. Either way, I am never going to please everyone. God created all of us as individuals with different gifts and abilities. Not everyone will embrace what we offer them. We need to live in the truth of Matthew 22:37 which states, "Jesus declared, 'Love the Lord your God with all your heart and with all your soul and with all your mind.'" Then we will be free to leave the rest up to God.

The first step in seeking out your worth is understanding the incorrect messages you have received from people in your life you are close to. We all receive incorrect messages, but it is how we individually address the messages given to us that sometimes defines us. I encourage you to not let your worth be dictated by the messages sinful people in your life have given to you. Don't be surprised when people in your life say or do hurtful things. Just forgive them and move on. They too need to work through their own incorrect messages people have given them. It does not matter if they know Jesus or not; they, too, have hurts. Understanding this and being mature enough to show grace will enable you to rise above the incorrect messages that have produced hurt through faith in our Savior, Jesus Christ. He alone can and will heal those hurts. It's not an easy task, but the more you work on this in your own life, the more you will shine like Jesus to those around you. Stay encouraged and look toward the truth, my dear sister. You are not alone in your journey!

Letter 3

*D*ear Discouraged,

Don't give up! I know you are struggling, but don't give up. I know life seems unfair. I know you wonder how you got to this point in life. I know you wonder if things will ever get any better. I know you feel defeated, but you are not! Let me share with you that if you know Jesus Christ as your personal Lord and Savior, life will get better. You see, this world we live in is not all there is to life. If we've given our heart over to Jesus Christ, we are not citizens of this present world. We are citizens of another kingdom. This is a kingdom that is built on a foundation that will never crumble, a kingdom that will not need demolition or repo because it is falling apart. It is a rock-solid kingdom based on the truth of God and His word. We know in John 17:17 that "God's word is truth." We can depend on this with all of our being. We can let go of the frustrations of our earthly kingdom to fully embrace and grab onto God's kingdom and experience His presence with us every day. We can allow God to lead us through this life and set our feet on solid ground. This is the treasure He offers us, which is access to God's kingdom. When we embrace what kingdom we are fighting for, we can realize victory.

Many times, I have asked my husband, Rick, "Why does it seem like I am so desperate for Jesus. Why can't I make it throughout a day without clinging to His feet with all that is in me?"

Rick's response to my question is always, "That's exactly where God wants all of us to be."

To which I respond, "It seems like some people can just go through their day without this desperation. It seems as if most of us know we need a Savior in Jesus, but do we really live that way?

The answer to this is obviously, "No." We try to live life without fully surrendering to God's plan for our lives. It becomes a battle of wills—our will versus God's will. We think that we have to protect or hold on to portions of our life without exposing them to the truth of God's word. Inevitably, our response is going to cause us total frustration. The answer is we need to surrender our will and our life to Him. I have learned that a part of allowing the fruit of the Spirit to be overflowing in my life means I need to give up building my own kingdom here on earth and, instead, live for His kingdom each and every day. In Galatians 5, we read that the fruit of the Spirit is love, joy, peace, patience, kindness, goodness, faithfulness, and self-control. There is no way on earth I could live this out every day on my own. That is why it is called the fruit of the Spirit. When the Spirit of God is alive in us, we will see this fruit overflowing in our lives, and those around us will be witness to it. We see God move in and through us in ways that point to His work, not ours. We begin to behave in ways that astonish even ourselves.

At the risk of being transparent, I would like to share with you how God accomplished His will in my life. It was not an easy process for me since I struggle with being stubborn. However, I would not trade the process for anything. I had a lot of head knowledge of Scripture, but it seemed to have a hard time working its way to my heart where I would then move it down to my feet to live it out in my everyday walk.

When my husband and I were going through the worst eighteen months of our marriage, we were in the process of losing our family business, our forever home we had built, our cars, our pride, and our reputation. Rick and I started a construction company a few years earlier. Rick had been working as vice president of a roofing company that started building homes, and I was a stay-at-home mom. Things were going well, and we had given birth to our third child, Maddie. We just moved in to a new home that Rick's company had built, and we were doing well. Then two weeks before Rick quit his job at the roofing company, God had laid it on my heart that maybe we would be starting our own company. Two weeks later, Rick came home from work and said he was going to do just that. He was leaving the company he worked for due to some decisions made by the owner that didn't sit well with him. He was going to start his own company. God had prepared my heart in advance, and we both agreed this was what we were called to do. So the journey began.

The next few years were challenging, but the business was moving along nicely. We built our dream home that we planned on retiring in, and all was well. We were building beautiful custom homes and had quite a few going at the time.

The downward spiral started for us when we were in the process of building a three-story home on a lake for a client. The project was moving along smoothly until that fateful day that summer. The client and Rick met at the construction site to talk about the project. The client was not happy with the speed the project was going. Rick could sense his irritability and laid out the ground rules. Rick shared with the client he was not to do anything on the construction site except for cleanup around the outside of the house. The client was obviously not happy with this. Rick made it clear what was expected and left to have lunch with the kids and I. The client chose to disregard Rick's rules and decided to take matters into his own hands. He proceeded to climb onto a machine that lifted materials up to the roof of the house for the roofer to use. It had been raining that day, and the ground was muddy. Immediately, the machine fell into the house, and the house came tumbling down. The man on the roof who was roofing the house ended up in the lake and, thankfully, did not die. He was rushed to the hospital with severe injuries. The authorities were also called. It was an awful scene. Rick and I received the call that the house had fallen while we were having lunch. Immediately, Rick left and headed to the construction site to observe the damage. It wasn't good. The next few months consisted of insurance companies arguing back and forth regarding who would pay for the damage since it was the homeowner who caused it, but Rick was the builder. All construction was halted until the insurance companies could hash it out. No bills were being paid, which then affected all of our other projects as well. Then without boring you with all the details, we were taken to court, and because of malpractice on the part of our attorney, we lost the case. This sent our business in a downward spiral we could not stop. We immediately began to pray about what we should do. Do we liquidate and shut down the business, or do we continue to try to make it work and see if we can work our way out of this huge hole we were in? As a stay-at-home mom, I had a lot of time, while the kids were in school, to pray. I don't think I've ever spent so much time on my knees.

The moment the house structure fell was the moment that set in motion a trajectory that would change our life, our marriage, the life of our kids, and our walk with the Lord. The next eighteen months became hell on earth as we tried to navigate through court proceedings, lawyers, contractors, etc. It was a time that was defining our future path. All of the ways we had used in the past to get us through hard times were not working. We used to turn to going out to eat to feel better. This didn't work because we had no money. We also used to turn to our friends and family for support, but the problem was too big for them to help with. This was a God-sized problem, and it had to have a God-sized answer.

Personally, I had not worked through any of my childhood junk yet. It was evident there was some serious pruning that needed to happen in my life as well as Rick's, and we were in for a ride. Much like a tree or plant is unable to bear fruit unless all of the dead branches and leaves are cut off, we were in a place where we needed those things in our lives that were in the way of the fruit of the Spirit overflowing to be cut off as well. It began to happen right before our eyes, and our friends and family had a front-row seat to watch. This was a ride that would show us what God created us for, a ride that would eventually destroy relationships and, surprisingly, create stronger ones. Our business affected so many people, and we were in for a beatdown by our worst enemy, Satan himself.

Our crumbling business was what Satan used to bring to the surface my feelings of unworthiness and shame from childhood. I became extremely depressed to the point of almost having a breakdown. I felt very hopeless and even suicidal at times. I needed not just Jesus as my Savior; I needed Him as my life. I needed to stop focusing on building my kingdom and get serious about building His eternal kingdom by valuing what He values, and that is pointing people to Him and giving His name glory, not my own name. I wanted to know exactly what God had to say about what we were going through, so I decided to go to a counseling/discipleship program in the city we lived in. It was life changing. Through this program, I learned what my true identity is, how to work through incorrect messages I receive from others, how to handle triggers that may come up, and ultimately, how to let go of my life to have Christ's life live through me. I began to live the life I was created to live for Jesus, even in the midst of extremely difficult circumstances. I began to let go of all of my rights that I thought I had—my right to a good reputation (remember, Christ did not have a good reputation with everyone), my right to comfort, my right to a good life, my right to presume my will on God's, and so on. Surrendering all of my rights was one of the most freeing things I have ever done. Holding onto our rights is one of the first steps in making Jesus Lord of our lives, and this was freeing to me. I was free to love as Christ loved. I was free to leave a legacy based on my walk with Jesus, not what we had or didn't have. I began living for God's kingdom, in the light of our earthly kingdom literally falling to the ground. My focus was now on how I could bring God glory in the midst of the trauma we were going through. My eyes became fixed on Jesus who gave me my faith.

My change in perspective came as a surprise to even me. I am not sure if you have ever had to deal with a bill collector, but they are relentless. They try to make you feel worthless and awful so you will pay your bill. We had been receiving these phone calls for months. Each time someone called, I would get so upset and feel so bad about myself and our situation. These calls would trigger my feeling of guilt and shame from my childhood which I still hadn't dealt with. Then I began to release the shame by understanding and praying through His love, mercy, and forgiveness for me. I also began to confess my sins and believe that Christ died on the cross for all of the shame and guilt I was carrying, and He wanted me to be released from these chains. I allowed Christ's life to live through me as a result, and I actually started witnessing to one of the bill collectors that called us. After a few minutes of me sharing Scripture and encouragement, the man shared with me that he and his wife were going through a bankruptcy. I was able to give him encouragement through Scripture. After he and I got off the phone, he called Rick and told him he had been encouraged by what I was sharing with him. This was only something God could do. On my own, I wouldn't have had the strength to have that type of conversation, but God showed me His strength through my weakness. This proved to be true that day, and I will never forget it. Hopefully, the man on the other end of the phone won't either.

God used what I thought was an ugly situation to show His people His power. We had numerous friends that had a front-row seat to watch God move and work in our lives. His faithfulness was profound, and it was pointing people to him. Some of our friends in our small group said to us that they were jealous of us. Their jealousy had nothing to do with Rick or I. It had everything to do with God's working in our lives. They were being drawn to him and were seeing Him because of our circumstance. Our faith was taken to a new level because of the pruning God was doing in us. Others around us were craving a sincere relationship with God.

Both Rick and I were moved to a point of having a settled confidence in what God was doing. We believed with all of our hearts that He had a plan, and we watched it unfold before our eyes. It was the sort of peace only God could give, and it was contagious. It was all Jesus! Once you've experienced His life and what His life offers, there is no going back.

Letter 4

$\mathcal{D}$ear Insecure,

Stop *comparing*! As women, some of our problems in life stem from our bad habit of comparing ourselves with others. It might be a comparison of what others have that we don't, what kind of job we have or don't have, what kind of money we have or don't have, or even what God is doing in our lives versus what He is doing in someone else's life.

In Luke 10, toward the end of the chapter, we read the story about Mary and Martha. Something about this story stood out to me the last time I read through it. Martha was comparing what she was doing with what Mary was doing for Jesus. Martha was not happy that she was doing all physical work, while Mary was sitting at Jesus feet. It was obvious Martha was not happy. I don't know one time in my life that

I have played the comparison game, and it grew my relationship with the Lord. On the contrary. It either made me feel proud about my situation, or it made me discontent. We see this in Martha. The way in which she was comparing herself with Mary led her to harboring bitterness.

Our society lives in a state of constant comparison. This is not only discouraging, at times, it is contrary to what God's word says. Comparing can lead to either pride or discontentment, which are both sinful. So what is the solution? I'll say it again, Jesus! The life He gave us through His death, burial, and resurrection provides us with everything we need. Many years ago, I decided to create a mission statement for my life. As I combed through scriptures in the Bible, searching for just the right verse to use in my mission statement, I came upon Matthew 5:3–12, which says,

> Blessed are the poor in spirit, for theirs is the kingdom of heaven. Blessed are those who mourn, for they will be comforted. Blessed are the meek, for they will inherit the earth. Blessed are those who hunger and thirst for righteousness, for they will be filled. Blessed are the merciful, for they will be shown mercy. Blessed are the pure in heart, for they will see God. Blessed are the peacemakers, for they will be called children of God. Blessed are those who are persecuted because of righteousness, for theirs is the kingdom of heaven. Blessed are you when people insult you, persecute you and falsely say all kinds of evil against you because of me. Rejoice and be glad, because great is your reward

in heaven, for in the same way they perse-
cuted the prophets who were before you.
(Matt. 5:3–12)

I love these verses. They demonstrate to me the way
I should be living every day. I love how the verses not only
describe the type of character and behavior we should have,
but it also gives us the outcome. For many years now, I have
prayed that my life would resemble these truths, but I have
failed many times because of being distracted by comparing
myself to others. I needed to refocus on the truth found in
my mission statement (Matt. 5:3–12). I have even sought to
memorize this passage so I can think of it often. Filling our
minds with verses that we individually need to claim can be
a way to battle comparison. When I realized what my personal mission statement is and what I am called to live like
as a follower of Christ, I made the conscious decision to not
worry about what is happening in other people's lives. That
is for God to handle. This does not mean I do not care about
other people and what is happening in their lives, but comparing their situation with mine can pose problems with my
relationship with God.

There were times when I chose to view someone as a
threat or a competitor. I did not realize this thought process was self-defeating and provided no way for me to be
Jesus to others. Instead, I chose to view others as no different
than myself who needs equal amounts of grace and mercy.
Changing the way I thought about other people took all the
pressure off me and provided opportunities for me to simply love them the way Jesus would want me to. Sometimes,
this meant giving up my right to be right, or my right to be
viewed as having it all together. I remember a time when
our children were young, and I was staying at home raising

them. I did a great job taking care of our home, even to a fault. When we would make plans with friends to have them over for dinner, I would spend countless hours cleaning and making sure our home was clean, neat, and looked perfect. On one occasion, a close friend of mine and her family came over for dinner, and when they left and arrived at home, her husband compared how I took care of our home with the way she took care of their home. I was obviously a clean freak, and she was not. What I realized after that incident was that my obsession with needing to be viewed a certain way actually negatively affected my close friend's marriage. I was convicted and decided this was something I needed to stop doing. Instead, I needed to let go of my right to be viewed as perfect, and just be me. This meant keeping a clean house was not going to be number one on my list every day. I was going to make relationships top priority.

I truly love the verses I listed from Matthew because they are attainable in life. We can live it out in our everyday lives, but we have to be intentional about it. Our tendency is not to be meek, pure in heart, or poor in spirit. The world we live in preaches a much different message to us. We are presented opportunities every day to live selfishly with pride. It is amazing how if I wake up in the morning thinking about these verses and meditate on them, it is much easier for me to be reminded and convicted to live by them. My response to situations that arise throughout the day looks very different than if my mind is not thinking about Matthew 5:3–12. These truths have become like a cloud by day and a fire by night. In the book of Exodus in the Bible, the Israelites followed a cloud by day and a fire by night when they left their years of slavery in Egypt. We read about this in Genesis. You see, God didn't just lead them out of slavery in Egypt to abandon them in the desert. On the contrary, He provided something for them to follow and lead them with. That's exactly what His Word provides us, and exactly what a personal mission statement does. We just have to open our eyes and take the time to read, meditate, and apply it to our lives. If the Israelites chose to close their eyes and look away from the cloud or fire because of fear or comparison, or the fact it was a little weird to follow a cloud and fire, they would not have been able to be led. If we are so busy comparing ourselves with everyone else and looking everywhere but where we need to look, which is at the face of Christ, then we will be lost and actually jeopardize our freedom from the slavery of sin. I have experienced firsthand the peace and joy God gives to those that live according to His leading.

This reminds me of when I was a child. At a very early age, I learned to compare myself to others. I was really insecure based on the dysfunction that was going on in our home. When I was six years old, my dad began soliciting my mom for sex. He had been struggling with an addiction to pornography, and it progressed to this point. My parents would be gone numerous nights a week, and then on Sunday, we attended a Baptist church where my dad led the music up front, and my mom taught Sunday school. You can imagine the confusion that was going on in our house, but more importantly, this produced insecurity, which birthed comparison. Many people have asked me if I understood what was happening at such a young age, and my answer is always no. I did not understand what was happening until I was in about fifth grade. I knew whatever was going on was not good due to the arguments going on between my parents as well as them being gone all night long. I would wake up in the morning and go into their bedroom to see if they had been sleeping in their bed. When their bed was made, I knew they were gone.

Every time this happened, my heart would sink. I knew in my heart things were not good. I think of this problem that existed as an unwanted guest in our home. I just wanted them to stay home at night. I just wanted them to stop fighting. I just wanted to be a normal family like all of my other friends and family. Other problems began to exist because of the decisions my parents were making. We had financial hardship. There was both physical and emotional abuse, and my mom would leave us and then come back, only to have it all start again. This was the cycle that ran our home. It was something I had to get used to because I had absolutely no control over any of it. All I could do was pray, and pray is what I did. From a very early age, I would beg God to make my parents stay home at night. I would plead with him every night before I fell asleep to make the unwanted guest in our home leave. However, He chose to allow it to continue until I was eighteen years old and graduating from high school. We were eventually kicked out of the church we attended and were ostracized by extended family and friends once they discovered what was going on in our home. This became a very lonely time in my life. This brought on so much discontent in me. I started presuming my will on God's will for my future. I did not trust His will for me based on what He was allowing to happen in our home. I decided to believe that I knew what was best for my life and would do everything in my power to make my will happen. This was not spiritually healthy for me to think this way, but I had no one speaking truth into my life. Nevertheless, it is how I coped. I determined that, at all cost, I was going to be accepted by people. I was going to avoid any more rejection from others if I could help it. This is when my people pleasing began. I learned that if I meet other people's needs, they would like me. In actuality, it was all about getting my own need for acceptance met.

Keep in mind, anything we find in this world that meets our needs outside of Christ is considered living out of our flesh, and it is sin. Even though I believed in God and Jesus as my personal Lord and Savior, I was getting my need for love and acceptance met from people pleasing, and it felt good. I could rely on this, so I thought. This all started in my mind with comparing and not liking the outcome.

Please know that I am not perfect and will never claim to be. Please do not let what God is doing in the lives of others defeat you or discourage you. Comparing starts in our minds, and that is where it needs to stop. He has a plan for you and your life even if it is hard to see right now. Please keep seeking Him and acknowledging His sovereign love for you.

Letter 5

$\mathcal{D}$ear Hopeless,

Don't lose hope! It seems as if there have been many opportunities in my life to lose hope. When I speak of losing hope, I am referring to my perception that whatever situation I am in, that I will never recover from it. The older I get and the more life I have lived, the harder it is for my initial reaction to a difficult situation to be hope versus discouragement and despair. However, this is a wrong perspective, no matter how much life I have lived. You see, the opposite could be true too. The older I get and the more life experiences I have lived, the more hope I should have. Even in the midst of a crisis, I have seen God's hand provide and protect me from that which seeks to destroy me. It is a choice. Much like everything in life, hope is a choice. We can choose to believe in it, or not. It is entirely up to us as individuals.

When I explained earlier about Rick and I being forced to walk away from our construction business, we had to decide what we were going to believe in—either what God says in His Word is true, or it is not. We can choose to have a hopeful perspective based on what we know about God's character and how He displays it. We had come to a crossroad in our life, and we were going to have to choose what to believe. For us, seeking another perspective took us hitting rock bottom, with nowhere to look but up—looking up to a God that had us in the palm of His hand, looking up to a God that knew we would be okay, and so would our children. This was not just about the situation of the moment, but it was about setting a new direction for the legacy we were going to leave to our children and grandchildren. It was one of knowing our identity is in Christ and loving Him with all that is in us. God knew our children needed more than a big beautiful home to live in with a nice comfortable life. They needed the example set by their parents of being desperate for Jesus. God not only showed Rick and I His faithfulness, but he showed it to our children as well. This was not just about building our testimony of God's faithfulness; it was also about building our children's as well. Our family values changed drastically from seeking perfection, money, and popularity as idols to seeking Jesus. You see, dear friend, anything we put above God in our lives is an idol. This meant we were now seeking to build His kingdom, not our own. It meant bringing God glory through the hard times as well as the good times. It meant loving other people more than we loved our things. It meant being obedient to God's will even if it offends those around us.

Sure, many times I have asked God why He would allow us to go through what we did. In my weak mind, it didn't bring Him glory. I wondered how not paying the bills could bring Him glory, and what I realized was that it may not have had everything to do with Rick and I. Maybe our obedience as we walked through what we thought was the valley of the shadow of death was also to prune other hearts as well. Again, our obedience does not guarantee everyone involved will experience a happy ending. This was a really hard pill for me to swallow as a person who struggled with people pleasing. There was plenty of unhappy people because of the demise of the company as I have discussed earlier. Not only did investors in our company lose money, but the contractors that we hired lost money, and we could not meet our financial obligations. I had to leave all of that at the foot of the cross. It was in His hands because He is God, and I am not. I love 1 Peter 5:10, where it says, "And the God of all grace, who called you to His eternal glory in Christ after you have suffered a little while, will himself restore you and make you strong, firm, and steadfast." This is a promise I have held on for years and encourage you to embrace it as well. It will provide you with much hope. There is a settled confidence that we can obtain having gone through major events in our lives. It is a settled confidence in Christ and His word.

Rick and I could have chosen to continue to wallow in the worries of how to pay bills, and how we were going to make it right with all those we owed money to as well as how we were going to "save face." We could have continued to spiral downward, which would have meant divorce, pain, and potential suicide. Yes, you heard me correctly, suicide. We had come to the end of our ropes, and we understood things had to change, and they had to change quickly. We were looking at our situation from a human perspective instead of a God perspective. However, we quickly realized it was important for us to choose to believe God's word is true.

God's word is true whether life is going great or circling the drain. God's word is true whether everyone around you likes you and thinks you are amazing, or everyone is upset with you. God's word is true whether you have a million dollars in your bank account or a measly five dollars. God's word is true if you own your home, or you're homeless. God's truth never changes. When those around me choose to discredit the amazing miracles God has displayed in my life, they are not hurting me, but they are outright denying the power of God in my life. It has nothing to do with what I have done but what He has done for me. This has become very disheartening to me, but again, I have a choice. I can choose to not listen to the naysayers in my life who continue to keep me down and discouraged (even believers) or I can choose to look at truth and be hopeful and celebrate His goodness in my life even amidst the seemingly unbearable situations He has allowed.

I love the story of Job for many reasons. One reason in particular is due to the fact that even though Job was found righteous, God still allowed Satan to attempt to discourage and destroy him using worldly means. Job had no idea that God was going to reward him twofold at the end of the book. We all celebrate with Job and think to ourselves what a great story. However, if you really contemplate the pain Job had to go through, it was incredible. This story should bring us so much hope, knowing that we are not privy to the end of our stories. We don't know what God has in store for us. Obviously, if we believe in Jesus as our Lord and Savior, we know we will live in eternity with God. However, we don't know our futures here on earth. That is why we must hold tight to the hope He plants within us. The hope is Jesus and the life that He offers us. In order to obtain this life, we must give him our own life in exchange. It is as if we hand Him our hearts, and He hands us all that He is. He gives us His forgiveness, His Spirit in us, His blessings, His promises, His peace, and so on. Once we make the exchange, we will then have the opportunity to live a life that shines and glorifies His name. If we can keep the perspective that He is our refiner, and the goal is for Him to see Himself in us and glorified, we will have chosen to have hope.

Letter 6

*D*ear Suffering Sister,

Please choose your identity wisely. All of us identify with something or someone in our life, and we take that on ourselves as being a part of who we are. Growing up in the home I did, I found my identity to be sports. At the time, I had no one speaking truth into my life except for what I received from the Christian school I was attending. My parents did not have much money at all, and yet they found it important to send me to a Christian school across town where many of the students came from very wealthy families. This was a God thing, and it was evident God was taking care of me.

As a young child, I was always involved with sports. We are a very athletic family, even dating back to my grandparents who were still golfing well into their eighties. As a kid, I was involved in softball leagues and would spend lots of time in the gym watching my dad play league basketball. I was naturally fast, so this helped me succeed. In middle school and high school, I worked hard at playing softball, basketball, and I did cheer as well. I learned a lot about team sports and how to be a team player, which continues to drive much of my perspective on good leadership. Because of this, I have the discernment and am able to spot someone who did not play team sports based on their ability to work as a team player. This was a blessing and made me some of who I am today. I loved going to school and participating in athletics because I was able to momentarily hide the intense inner pain I was dealing with on a daily basis. I deeply wanted to be needed, accepted, and normal, and I could do this at school and in sports. I learned to hide the pain well. Not many people knew what was going on in our home. Even my closest friends had no idea what was happening in my family.

It wasn't until college that I shared what was happening in my home with my best friend. We had been friends for quite a few years, and our families were friends as well. She was shocked and amazed that I was able to hide it that well. It just goes to show that you can never judge a book by its cover. I wanted to choose my own identity, and I thought that by being a good athlete, I would be accepted and loved not only by my parents but those at school as well. But what was going to happen when I stopped playing sports? Then what would I identify with? At that point in my life, I moved on to perfectionism and overachieving.

I graduated from college in three and a half years and found a job right away. Rick and I got married soon after that and began to work on the perfection thing together. Rick was actually pretty good at it too, so we were quite the pair. It was important to look perfect, to work toward owning a beautiful home, nice cars, and beautiful, perfect kids. Both Rick and I were very involved in our church as well. From the outside, we looked like the family that had it all together. I would even shop at a local boutique and buy matching outfits for all three of our children. Then on Sunday, when we went to church together, we were all matching. This became our identity. It wasn't until the collapse of our business that our glass house shattered. Praise God for this! He was able to take the broken glass and put it back together the way He wanted to. Through our pain, we identified with Christ, His suffering, and His life. My life verse became Galatians 2:20, which states, "I have been crucified with Christ therefore I no longer live, but Jesus Christ lives in me. And the life that I now live in the flesh I live by faith in the Son of God who loves me and gave Himself for me."

My identity had changed. The chains of this world that I was dragging with me everywhere I went were gone. They were broken, and my relationship and fellowship with Christ looked very different. I grew to learn what my flesh was, and how to get rid of it. Again, our flesh is our way of getting our needs met outside of Jesus Christ. I was able to recognize what these were and deal with them. I felt so much freedom! Living in the world quickly began to feel like I was a fish swimming upstream. The things that used to be so important to me no longer mattered anymore. The pressures of having money and looking perfect were gone. I realized quickly that money did not equal righteousness. I was a child of God and knew it without a shadow of a doubt, and my identity was in Him. There was no going back. I soon began to grasp that whatever my parents had chosen to do with their life had nothing to do with me and my identity. Their decisions did not dictate my identity. My decisions did not even dictate my identity. Instead, Christ dictated my identity.

Walking in this new identity now meant I had to change some things in my life to continue in the freedom Christ gave me through His death on the cross. One of the things I needed to do was forgive my parents for the hellish child-hood they created for me. I knew that forgiveness was part of my identity in Christ, and if I wanted to be forgiven for all of my ugly sins, I needed to forgive them. This has easily been one of the most difficult things God has asked me to do. I wanted to punish them. I wanted them to pay for what they did to me and my brothers. I wanted them to hurt like I hurt. But this was not what was expected of me now. God chose me as His child, and it was time for me to look differ-ent from the world. The world would tell me that I had every right to be angry. However, now it was time to lay that hurt at the cross and forgive them. You see, in Ephesians 2:9, it says, "Not by works, so that on one can boast." Our salvation was not based on anything we have done or could do, and all of our sin was on Jesus while He hung on the cross. Our wonderful identity from Christ was a free gift that we only have to accept. Living in that identity depends on our ability to have faith that "God's word is truth" (John 17:17), and that He is who He says He is. Spending time in His word and in prayer is critical to understanding and embracing this identity so that we can live our lives on pointing people to Jesus and giving Him glory. Sometimes, this means doing the hard stuff like forgiving, even when everyone else says you have every right not to.

I love the movie *Finding Nemo*. There is a part in the movie where the female fish sings over and over, "Just keep swimming, just keep swimming." I love this. This is exactly what we have to do in this life. Keep swimming upstream. Keep your eyes on the one who created you, and because of your testimony, others may "taste and see that the Lord is good" (Psalm 34:8). We know in 2 Timothy 2:12, "If we deny Him, He also will deny us." I know that when I stand at the entrance to heaven, I don't want Him to deny me. This is a pretty clear call for us to swim upstream. Don't be fearful of this call. Embrace it and live in your true identity!

Letter 7

$\mathcal{D}$ear Control Freak,

Many people have looked at my life with disbelief. I have actually been told, "You don't remember any memories of growing up. You were young." Well, let me tell you that the things that went on in our home were horrific. What happened in our home was not something I just forget. The memories are ingrained in my mind and, to some extent, in my heart. They are a part of who I am. They have given me a love for people that are struggling with hurt, trauma, abuse, and disappointment. I believe God allowed me to go through certain life experiences because He knew I would be willing to be His hands and feet to those who are hurting. However, I had to go through some intense healing to get to the point where I could even talk about what happened to me. I had to let the pain and trauma go so God could take it and heal it. I had to let go of my control over my life and those around me. This was not easy, but the blessings on the other side of healing have been indescribable.

The peace and joy we receive from God when we choose to give our whole heart (including the pain and hurt) to Him is beyond words. I am sharing this with you because I have experienced it firsthand. I had to let go of my ability to control every detail of my life and realize there is freedom in not having to control everything. I had been hurt by the people closest to me, and I wanted to protect myself from letting that happen again. I was putting up relational walls that were self-destructive. I was only hurting myself by withdrawing from close relationships with people. No one is perfect, and neither am I. This was stemming from my desire to control my life. I had to learn to step out and trust imperfect people, including myself. This meant giving up the ability to control everything that happens to me. I began to trust God to protect my heart from hurt. However, I had to let go of my right to be hurt and know if He allowed hurt to happen to me, he would heal it as well. Remember, I had exchanged my heart for His life, so He holds my heart in His hands.

I experienced some of my deepest pain in life during some of the most formative years of my life. I lived with both the prostitute and pimp. It is difficult to even write this, but it is a critical part of my story. For many years, I lived with the shame that went along with this. However, I realized as I was going through the healing process, I don't have to, and neither do you. We do not own anyone else's issues and decisions. They may affect us, but they don't have to define us. Each of us has our own issues that we come to terms with. When we turn our focus intently on allowing God to teach us and mold us through the study of his Word, instead of focusing on other people's issues, we can grow in our fellowship with Him and become more like Him. This may mean setting up boundaries with others around you so you are able to be healthy. Those people that adhere to the boundaries you have set up are those you can have healthy relationships with.

We all have our own sin to deal with and our own issues to overcome, so why should we borrow trouble and stress by taking on someone else's issues as our own. This does not mean we won't pray for those who are struggling or "carry one another's burdens" as stated in Galatians 6:2. However, there is a difference between carrying their burdens and taking them on yourself. When I envision this, I see someone who is carrying a bag full of groceries. This bag is full of groceries that have yet to be eaten. However, when you get home from the store, you may consume some of the groceries you were carrying. You are not just carrying the groceries, but they are inside your body, and they have become a part of you. They are either going to make you healthy or sick, depending on what you choose to ingest. My point is this, the food is inside of your body. Because you have eaten it, and it is inside of your body, it will affect you in one way or another. When we simply carry one another's burdens, it is not affecting us one way or another like when we carry the bag of groceries. We are simply holding it for someone until we lay it at the feet of the cross through prayer. This is a healthy way to function as we are in relationship with others who are hurting. It's realizing we don't have the capacity to fix someone else and, instead, bringing it to the one who actually can, Jesus. We all have a Savior that is sitting at the right hand of God pleading on our behalf. Because we do, we can trust that when we pray, He hears us. He may not answer our prayers the way we want Him to, but I am reminded of Isaiah 55:8 that states,

"For my thoughts are not your thoughts, neither are your ways my ways." We can trust that He knows what's best for us and for those we love. We have to be careful not to try to be God or the Holy Spirit in the lives of those we love, but simply point them to Him.

Being a control freak did not produce what I have desired in life. I am learning to let go of the rights I think I am entitled to and embrace the freedom that comes from having a settled confidence in the perfect work of God in my life. Letting go of my right to control the circumstances in both my life and others has been a battle. Letting go of my right to have an easy and comfortable life has been a battle. Letting go of my right to be right all the time has been a battle. Letting Christ do anything with me, in me, and through me has been a battle. Every day, I have to wake up and intentionally let go all of my rights so I can allow the Holy Spirit to move me and work in me to follow God's will for me. This is no easy venture. Especially when a situation comes up throughout the day that challenges me and pushes me to claim my rights. Hopefully, the more I intentionally give up my rights, the easier it will get to live this out every day.

Letter 8

*D*ear Miserable Sister,

Choose your values wisely. Many people, whether Christian or not, go through life without understanding what they personally believe or, in other words, their personal value system. Values are actually what drive what you do or don't do as you live your life. We can actually choose to do things in our lives that act in contradiction to what our values actually are. For example, we may choose a job just because the pay is really high. It might be a job that we really don't like, and we are miserable. At this point, a decision needs to be made. Do we value the money we make or the ability to enjoy the job we go to every day? When our values are not lining up with our decisions, we typically become unsatisfied or discontent. There is usually some sort of feeling indicator that tells us we are not living congruent to our values. Sometimes, we push through it because we think that is what we are supposed to do, and other times, we choose to change the direction we are going and align our decisions with our values.

A perfect example of this in my life happened with my job. I was working a great paying job for a while, but not necessarily doing something I felt called to do. It was merely a paycheck. I thought it would be okay because I could just fill in the ministry need in my life by volunteering at church or at another organization in town. However, I realized quickly that was not what I was called to do. I was miserable every day I went to work. I realized I valued making a difference in people's lives more than I value bringing home a large paycheck that will give me the toys I want (building my kingdom).

I remember when Rick and I were going through the horrible eighteen months of losing the business. I was in so much emotional pain and was frustrated that no one knew what I was going through. None of my friends had ever gone through something like this before, and some of them were even putting blame on Rick and I. This was extremely hurtful as we felt like we were waiting on God to give us direction, and some could not understand that. They wondered why we were not doing more. They wanted us to fix it when we knew it was a God-sized problem that was going to take a God-sized answer. Well, one day, I was cleaning the bathroom floor on my hands and knees. At the same time, I was listening to music, and the song sung by Casting Crowns, "Can Anybody Hear Her," came on. It was so powerful! The chorus says:

> Does anybody hear her?
> Can anybody see?
> Or does anybody even know she's going
> down today?

Under the shadow of our steeple
With all the lost and lonely people
Searching for the hope that's tucked away
    in you and me
Does anybody hear her?
Can anybody see?

This song expressed exactly how I was feeling and have felt most of my life. I have felt like I could really never bring my hurts to church with me to be healed because I would be judged. My hurts were not what the church wanted to see. It was too messy. They feel unequipped to help me, and yet all I wanted was to feel loved and accepted by God's people. All I wanted was for someone to say that they care enough to walk alongside of me without judging me. At the moment this song came on, I knew what my calling was and is. It is to reach women who are hurting—women whom the church does not want to mess with like the woman at the well listed in Scripture. These are the women Jesus wants to reach. They know they need Jesus! They are desperate for Him because they have no one else, and nothing else. They know they can't earn their salvation and really don't have the capacity to try. They just know they need Jesus. This is so beautiful to me.

Many times, I have been that woman at church that was seeking love from God's people. I remember as a teenager living at home, my mom had left my dad because she was tired of going out at night, so it was just my dad, my younger brother, and me living in the house. My older brother was away at college at the time. We were attending a church around the corner, and I was involved with the youth group. My dad had approached the youth pastor's wife to see if she would take me under her wing and mentor me, and she said *no*. This was crushing. I felt as though I was not good enough to be loved by those in church. Well, it took me awhile to get over that, but I did. Then as an adult, I finally came to the spot in my walk with the Lord where I wanted to start using my story to point people to Jesus. I felt the Lord prodding me to become involved with the sex trafficking ministry at our church. This was a huge step for me, and I knew I was ready. God had been preparing me for many years, and I had gone through much healing.

I was asked to give my testimony in a video in front of the church. I did just that, and once the video was shown, I did not hear from anyone in the church. No one reached out to make sure I was doing okay or to encourage me. Even those in the specific area of ministry did not reach out. After two months went by, I met with one of the leaders of the church to let them know that they should probably not put someone in front of church to share and then leave them out to dry. He shared with me, "The church is not ready to handle this sort of thing yet." I really struggled with this because they had a so-called ministry to these types of people. Yet, I felt like I was not good enough to be loved or good enough to be an active part of the ministry. This had been my life, and it was brushed under the table as if I never lived through it and survived. It was very confusing and very hurtful.

This incident actually set my mind on a journey of trying to decide if I wanted to be called a "Christian" anymore. I was so disappointed in the church. It seemed like it was just the "popular" ministry to be a part of. They did not have any ministry to me at all. In fact, they practically turned me away from church. However, I decided to forgive again and realize the church is made up of people who need Jesus just as much as everyone else, and sometimes more. They are sinners just like everyone else. I wanted God to show me mercy and forgiveness, so it was important for me to show this to those in my church. This was really difficult, but I still knew my calling, and I was going to continue to pursue this calling.

That was when I took a job at the local homeless shelter. I knew I would be working with women who were on drugs, abused, neglected, lost, and even trafficked. I was ready. God had prepared me for this moment. So I left my great-paying job and began doing the job that fit within my values. You see, my values include empowering women who are hurting, more than making money. I enjoy comfort, but I am called to serving hurting women. I am willing to give up comfort for the lives of these women. They need to know they are worth that.

I encourage you to pray about your calling and create your own values to drive what you do every day. Don't get discouraged if it doesn't happen right away. Please keep trusting God has a plan, and He created you for that plan. It did not happen for me overnight. It took many years of waiting to finally move into what He has called me to do. It is a process. I can't wait to see what more lies ahead for me as I continue to seek hard after Him. I encourage you to do the same.

Letter 9

*D*ear Warrior,

As I write my final letter to you, I want to share one more thing. Don't turn away from the hard stuff. Don't try to dodge it or get out from under it. Instead, dive head first into your struggles and create your own battle plan for having victory. Lay it out ahead of time because the battle will come. Your battle is probably different than mine, and that is okay. Each of us is different. However, one thing should be part of your battle plan, and that is putting on the full armor of God. This will prove to protect you. We find an explanation of the full armor in Ephesians 6 in the Bible. It specifically describes the protection of our head, our chest, a shield, a sword, a belt, and boots. Pray through these elements every day and put them on before you get out of bed in the morning. Then you can know you are protected from the fiery darts Satan will try to shoot your way.

Our spiritual battle is no different than an earthly battle. The difference is the armor we put on looks different, and we can't see our enemy. Stay in the fight, my dear sister. Don't lose hope and give up. Our heavenly Father has blessings beyond measure for those that are faithful and stay in the battle. The blessing may only be eternal, but don't forget we are not here to build our personal, earthly kingdoms. We are here to build God's eternal kingdom of which we are citizens.

A second piece of your battle plan should be recognizing your flesh and sin. Recognize those things in life that you use, instead of Jesus, to meet your needs. Once you know what they are, you can battle them with prayer and Scripture. Be careful not to suppress them, thinking this will not harm you. At some point in your life, they will surface, and you will have to deal with them and expose them to the light. Lay them at the foot of the cross and leave them there. The victory is God's, so let's claim it.

Also, remember your true identity in Christ. Satan will try to maneuver his way into your thoughts to get you to question this. Don't do it. Don't question who you are in Christ. Stand firm in these truths. Don't forget, it is Christ in you who will give you the strength you need to win the battle. Just like the story in the Bible of David and Goliath. Don't be surprised when you experience victory in ways that you have never seen before. That is who God is. He gave the

Israelites victory over Goliath and his people through David, the shepherd boy with a sling and a stone. Amazing! Trust His strength in you. Don't live off your feelings. Live off the truth of God's Word. Study it with all that is in you, and pray so much you have bruises on your knees. And finally, create your mission statement and live according to this.

I know you have been hurt, and life has handed you lemons. It's not too late to make lemonade. You have a story to share, just like I do. We have been given a treasure in Jesus, and people need to know He can reach them no matter what they have done. They are still worth saving, and we know this because we have experienced extreme pain and yet have been able to find our Lord and Savior Jesus Christ. I encourage you to use your pain to help others navigate to Jesus. There is always a reason for our pain, and He will show you what that is if you ask Him. Be patient and continue to heal. I love that one of God's name is Jehovah Rapha, the God who heals. He absolutely does, and it's not just physically. He is healing you every day, just like He is healing me. Once you've experienced your healing, use your testimony to encourage others. Each of our testimonies can be stewarded to encourage others and point them to Jesus. One caution as you prepare to share, and that is to be careful not to point people to you and let it feed your need to be appreciated. It is really easy to succumb to and can be extremely destructive. In 2 Corinthians, chapter 1, Paul talks about comforting others with the comfort we get from God. When we understand other people's pain because of our own pain, we can authentically comfort them. It is not about us. It is about God and others. Let's keep this at the center of sharing our testimonies.

So just as I have taken a leap of faith in sharing some of my story, I challenge you to not turn away from what role God may ask you to play in building His kingdom. Don't get distracted by your pain or your success. Keep your eyes on Jesus, the author and finisher of your faith. There are people that need to hear stories of great hope, and your story may be just that. Don't turn away because you think it's too hard. That is when God's strength kicks in, and He accomplishes much through you. Don't believe the lies that the enemy will attempt to throw at you to discourage you. Satan will seek to discourage you. So count on it, figure out a battle plan, and move forward. I pray that your heart will be filled with all the goodness God can give. Don't give up when it gets hard. Let God bless you amidst the pain, and watch Him work. Then proclaim His glory to those who will listen. Let's not let the hardship and trials that are left behind in the wake of our journey dictate what is ahead for us. Let's be conquerors together. Let's not just survive, my dear sister, let's conquer and win!

About the Author

*L*isa loves spending time with her husband of twenty-five years, her two sons, her daughter, and her daughter-in-law. She resides in Richland, Washington, and moved across country twice. Lisa has a passion for working with women who are hurting. She has served on women's ministry boards as well as led Bible studies and mentored many women. She has worked for more than one nonprofit and has been awarded the Washington State University Women of Distinction. Lisa's main focus in life is to use her story, her gifts, and her passions to point others to Jesus. She has experienced firsthand the healing hand of Jehovah Rapha in her life. Her hope is to encourage women to understand and embrace that they are not alone in life.